HAVE FUN COOKING

with CHEF KEEP-IT-REAL

Dwayne Houston

HAVE FUN COOKING with CHEF KEEP-IT-REAL

COOKING
WITH A TWIST

XULON PRESS

Xulon Press
2301 Lucien Way #415
Maitland, FL 32751
407.339.4217
www.xulonpress.com

Paperback ISBN-13: 978-1-66284-971-8
Ebook ISBN-13: 978-1-66284-972-5

✳✳✳

Introduction

Cooking with Chef Keep-It-Real was inspired by God and my wife of over thirty-three years. She would egg me on to be creative when it came to making certain everyday dishes for breakfast, lunch, and dinner.

When taking a creative approach to cooking, we make it fun and enjoyable for all involved. Even our children enjoy making and creating their own special dishes, like Hell's Fire hot buffalo wings, and Twang Chicken, to name a couple. God has connected our family together like never before through something as simple as cooking.

As you begin to use these proven recipes that have worked for us, and that have been passed down to generations of family, friends, and loved ones, have fun in bringing lots of love to your home and kitchen.

❋·❋·❋
About the Author

Hi, my name is Dwayne Houston. I was born in Detroit, Michigan and came from a family of seven siblings; being able to cook was a must in our household. Each of us brothers and sisters had to learn to fend for ourselves. I remember every Thanksgiving: all eight of us would have to learn how to cook a dish. My mother would stand around, telling each one of us what ingredients to add to each item that was being cooked.

I got married in 1988 at the age of twenty-six to my wife of thirty-three years. I started a family of my own and began passing down recipes to my children. This book is inspired by my wife and children, after seeing how passionate I was about cooking. This book has been long overdue for many years, so I hope you enjoy many of our family's tried and proven recipes. Let's have fun cooking with a twist, with me, **Chef-Keep-It Real.**

※ ※ ※
A Word to the Wise

Meaning you!

All recipes may differ in temperature depending on the types of stoves, ovens, and grills you may have. All recipes in this cookbook were cooked on an electric stove or grill.

Please make sure to wash and clean all meats and vegetables to prevent the spread of gems and other bacteria. You may also want to use a meat temperature gauge to check the cores of your meats. A good rule of thumb is 160 degrees to kill germs and bacteria.

Also, keep in mind that all recipes may vary in taste depending on the types of sweetener, oils, milks, and seasoning you may use. [All ingredients are optional.]

Always remember: when working with children in the kitchen, let's make it a safe and enjoyable place to be. Please make sure that when handling hot items, your child wears heat-proof gloves or mittens to prevent burns, and always practice safety first!

"A family that cooks together loves to eat together."

❄❄❄

Cooking Measurement Abbreviations

U.S. units	Alternative U.S. units	Metric units
1-tsp	⅓ tbsp	5 ML
1-tbsp.	3 tsp or ½ fl oz	15 ML
¼-cup	4 tbsp or 2 fl oz	60 ML
⅓-cup	5 tbsp + 1 tsp	80 ML
½-cup	8 tbsp or 4 fl oz	125 ML
¾-cup	12 tbsp or 6 fl oz	180 ML
1-cup	16 tbsp or 8 fl oz	250 ML
1-pint	2 cups	500 ML
1-quart	4 cups or 2 pints	950 ML
1-gallon	8 pints, 4 quarts, or ½ peck	3.8 L
2-gallons	8 quarts or 1 peck	7.5 L
1-peck	¼ bushel or 2 gallons	8.8 L
4-pecks	1 bushel or 7 ¾ gallons	35.2 L

✳ ✳ ✳

Weight Measurements

g—gram
kg—kilogram
lb—pound
mg—milligram
oz—ounce

Other Measurement Units

doz—dozen
Lg—large
p—pinch
pkg—package
sm—small
sp—speck

Other Measurements

Bu—bushel
C—cup
Fl oz—fluid ounce
Gal—gallon
ML—milliliter
L—liter
Pk—peck
Pt—pint
Qt—quart
Tbsp—tablespoon
Tsp—teaspoon
Dsp—dessertspoon [in Australia]

NOTES

❊❊❊
Table of Contents

NOTES

Twang Chicken
Honey Apple Chicks

Makes seven servings

35 pieces wing dings
3 whole green apples
¼ cup honey
1 teaspoon onion powder
1 teaspoon garlic powder
½ teaspoon paprika
½ teaspoon salt and pepper

PREPARATION

Rinse each piece of chicken thoroughly and place on a large baking sheet. Season chicken with onion powder, garlic powder, paprika, salt and pepper, and combine well.

Slice apples into 2-inch pieces, and spread generously over chicken. Add honey over chicken and apples, making sure to cover all pieces.

PREHEAT OVEN [350 DEGREES]

Place chicken in baking sheet with aluminum foil, and place in hot oven, making sure to stir occasionally so that chicken will not stick. Let chicken cook for 30 to 45 minutes or until chicken is tender; remove from oven and let cool for 5 to 10 minutes and serve.

✳✳✳
Hell's Fire
Hot Buffalo Wings
Makes seven servings

35 pieces wing dings
2 cups flour
48 oz [1.5 qt] cooking oil
1 stick butter
1½ cup hot sauce
¼ cup tabasco sauce
½ tablespoon ground red pepper

PREPARATION

Rinse each piece of chicken thoroughly, place in a large bowl, and mix in red pepper, then sit to the side. While chicken is sitting, pour cooking oil in a large deep fryer and set to medium heat, about [350 F]. While oil is getting hot, pour flour into mixing bowl with chicken and mix well, covering all pieces of chicken. Carefully place into hot cooking oil; place about 10 to 12 pieces in fryer at a time. Cook for 10 to 15 minutes or until chicken is golden brown; after all chicken is done, set aside.

PREHEAT OVEN [350 DEGREES]

In a medium-size saucepan, combine hot sauce, tabasco sauce, and butter, cooking until butter is melted. Mix chicken in sauce [making sure every piece is fully covered]. Place the wing dings onto a baking pan, cover with foil tightly, and place into oven for 30 minutes or until chicken is tender; remove from oven and let sit for 3 to 5 minutes and serve.

Teriyaki
Baked Chicken

Makes five to six servings

10 to 12 pieces of chicken
½ cup teriyaki marinade sauce
¼ cup Worcestershire sauce
¼ cup hot sauce
½ teaspoon lemon pepper
½ teaspoon onion powder
½ teaspoon garlic powder

PREPARATION

Rinse all pieces of chicken thoroughly. Let water drain off and pat dry with paper towel. Lightly season with lemon pepper, onion powder, and garlic powder. Place chicken in a large bowl; pour in teriyaki marinade, hot sauce, and Worcestershire sauce. Mix all ingredients well with chicken, and let sit 30 to 60 minutes, letting marinade soak into chicken.

PREHEAT OVEN [375 DEGREES]

After chicken has set for the allotted time, place each piece into a large baking pan and cover with foil tightly. Cook for about 30 to 45 minutes, or until all the pinkness is gone from chicken. Remove from oven and let sit for 3 to 5 minutes and serve.

✳ ✳ ✳

Mr. D's Chicken
Done Right

Makes six servings

24 pieces of chicken wing dings
2 ½ cups flour
48 oz [1.5 qt]
½ teaspoon lemon pepper
½ teaspoon garlic powder
½ teaspoon onion powder
1 teaspoon mustard
¼ cup hot sauce

PREPARATION

In a large bowl, combine flour, lemon pepper, garlic powder, and onion powder. Rinse chicken well in cool water, drain, and pat dry with paper towel. Place chicken in another large bowl; combine mustard and hot sauce with chicken.

FRY

Pour cooking oil into a deep fryer and set to medium heat [350 degrees].

While oil is getting hot, place pieces of chicken into flour, covering each piece well. Carefully place chicken into hot oil, no more than 10 to 12 pieces at a time. Cook for 10 to 15 minutes or until chicken is golden brown. When chicken is done, place on a pan, covered with paper towel, so that oil may drain.

You may serve while hot or let sit until chicken has cooled down.

※ ❋ ※

Chicken and Shrimp Stir Fry
Hot and Spicy

Makes four to five servings

1 ½ cups chicken broth
3 tablespoons teriyaki sauce
2 tablespoons cornstarch
¼ teaspoon ground red pepper
½ pound boneless skinless chicken breast
1 tablespoon minced garlic
2 tablespoons vegetable oil
½ pound raw shrimp
2 cups chopped frozen broccoli
½ cup sliced mushrooms
1 small red bell pepper
1 small onion

PREPARATION

In a medium bowl, combine chicken broth, teriyaki sauce, cornstarch, minced garlic, and ground red pepper. Set aside, peel, and rinse shrimp and set aside. Also, rinse chicken in a large frying pan; put in 1 tablespoon of oil. Add chicken, cooking until all pinkness is gone; add shrimp; cook until shrimp turn pink. Add broccoli, mushrooms, onion, and bell pepper into pan and cook for 3 to 5 minutes or until vegetables are crisp and tender; remove from heat and serve with rice or noodles.

✳ ✴ ✳

Curry Chicken

Makes three to five servings

3 tablespoon vegetable oil
3 roman tomatoes
1 medium onion
2 ½ cups water
5 tablespoon curry powder
½ teaspoon ground red pepper
2 cups all propose flour
20 pieces of chicken wing dings

DEEP FRY [375 DEGREES]

Rinse all chicken thoroughly; pat dry with paper towel. Season [20 pieces] with your favorite seasoning.

Place flour into large bowl; lightly coat chicken with flour. After cooking oil is hot, carefully place chicken pieces into fryer for about 10 to 15 minutes or until golden brown. After chicken is done, set aside.

CURRY GRAVY

In a large frying pan, put 3 tablespoons of vegetable oil. Chop up 1 medium onion into small pieces. Place onion into hot oil over medium heat; cook until onions are golden brown. Chop tomatoes into 1-inch pieces; add tomatoes into pan, with onions cooking tomatoes until they are soft. Add 2 ½ cups water, 5 tablespoon curry powder, ½ teaspoon ground red pepper, and stir well. Add chicken to pan and mix well; let mixture come to a hard boil and cover with tight lid. Reduce heat to low and let simmer, stirring about every 15 minutes, until curry gravy thickens You may add more curry powder as needed. After curry has tightened and chicken is tender, you may serve over a hot bed of rice.

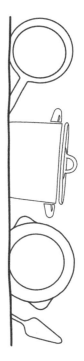

✹✺✹
Baked Tilapia
Lemon and Garlic Flavor

Makes six to eight servings

2 pounds of tilapia [filleted]
¼ teaspoon salt
¼ teaspoon lemon pepper
¼ teaspoon garlic powder
¼ teaspoon onion powder
½ cup lemon juice

PREPARATION

Wash and clean fish fillets with chilly water; drain and pat dry with paper towel. Combine salt, lemon pepper, garlic powder, and onion powder; sprinkle seasoning on both sides of fish.

PREHEAT OVEN [375 DEGREES]

Place each piece of fish on a large baking sheet, then brush each fish on both sides with lemon juice. Cover pan tightly with foil and place into oven. Cook for about 15 to 20 minutes or until fish is white and flakey; remove from heat and serve.

Salmon Patties
Golden Brown

Makes six to eight servings

1 can of pink salmon [14.75oz]
¼ cup chopped onion
¼ cup chopped green bell pepper
¼ teaspoon lemon pepper
¼ teaspoon garlic powder
1 large egg
¼ cup cornmeal
¼ cup cooking oil

PREPARATION

Open can of pink salmon; drain all water in a medium bowl. Chop up salmon until all chunks are gone, then combine onion, green bell pepper, lemon powder, and garlic powder into bowl. Mix well; add beaten egg and cornmeal, making sure all ingredients are mixed well.

FRY

In a 12-inch frying pan, pour in cooking oil; heat to medium. Roll salmon into golf ball-sized balls and then flatten with hand. Carefully place into hot oil, letting them cook for 3 to 5 minutes, or until golden brown on both sides. Remove from pan and let sit on paper towel so that oil will drain; let cool or serve hot [great with rice].

✳✳✳

Southern Fried
Catfish Fillets

Makes four to six servings

12 catfish fillets
2 ½ cups cornmeal [fish seasoning optional]
48 oz bottle cooking oil
¼ teaspoon salt
¼ teaspoon black pepper
¼ teaspoon onion powder
¼ teaspoon garlic powder

PREPARATION

In a large bowl, mix cornmeal, salt, pepper, onion powder, and garlic powder together well. Wash all pieces of fish fillets in chilly water; pat dry with paper towel.

PREHEAT DEEP FRYER [350 DEGREES]

Pour cooking oil into fryer and heat to [350 degrees]. While oil is getting hot, place each piece of fish into cornmeal mix one at a time, making sure to cover both sides of fish. Make sure not to put more than 4 to 5 pieces of fish in fryer at a time; cook for 10 to 15 minutes or until golden brown on both sides, or fish is white and flaky on the inside. After fish is done, place on a pan that is covered with a paper towel so that oil will drain off fish. Let sit or serve while hot. Great with fries and coleslaw.

☀❊☀
Chicken Quesadillas

Makes four to five servings

1 cup pre-cooked chicken breast
½ cup chunky salsa
1 pack flour tortillas [8-inches]
2 cups shredded Colby-jack cheese
¼ cup sour cream
1 can of cooking spray

PREPARATION

Place precooked chicken in a medium bowl; add salsa and mix well. In a 9-inch nonstick pan, spray cooking spray and place flour tortillas in pan over medium heat. Layer chicken mix with salsa and cheese; add other layer of tortillas and spray with cooking spray. Cook on one side for about 2 minutes or until golden brown, then carefully turn tortillas and repeat on other side. This method will work for all remaining tortillas; remove from pan and cut into four wedges. Add sour cream and salsa as desired.

﹡﹡﹡

Chicken Salad
Sandwich

Makes six to eight servings

4 pieces boneless, skinless chicken breast
¼ cup of chopped [finely] onion optional
¼ cup of chopped [finely] celery
¼ teaspoon salt
1 ½ teaspoon garlic powder
2 tablespoon melted butter
½ cup mayonnaise
¼ cup of dried cranberries
¼ cup of sliced grapes

PREPARATION

Thoroughly rinse all pieces of chicken. Cut chicken into bite-sized pieces; in a large pan, place butter, chicken, salt, and garlic powder over medium heat, cooking until all pinkness is gone and chicken is easy to pull apart. After chicken is done, let drain until it has cooled all the way down. Place chicken in a large bowl; add chopped onion, celery, grapes, dried cranberries, and mayonnaise; if needed, add more mayonnaise. Mix well, then place in refrigerator and let chill. After chilling, make sandwiches or serve with crackers; also goes great with croissants.

✳❀✳

Hardy Chicken and Dumpling
Creamy and Good

Makes ten to twelve servings

6 cups water

32 oz box chicken broth

4 to 5 boneless, skinless chicken breasts

1 can cream of chicken [26 oz can]

1 1/2 cup chopped celery

1 box rolled dough [pie crust 2 pack]

2 cups frozen mixed vegetables

½ teaspoon lemon pepper

½ teaspoon onion powder

½ teaspoon garlic powder

1 tablespoon vegetable oil

PREPARE CHICKEN

Rinse chicken breast, then cut each one into ½ inch cubes. In a large 5-quart pot, put in 1 tablespoon of oil; add chicken. Cook over medium heat until chicken is done. Add water, broth, and all other ingredients besides dough and cream of chicken. Bring to hard broil; place lid and reduce heat to medium. Add cream of chicken and bring back to broil.

PREPARE DUMPLINGS

While waiting on other ingredients to cook, unroll dough crust and cut into 1-inch squares. Carefully add dough pieces into soup mixture, stirring as you drop them. Cover with lid once again and reduce heat until dumplings rise to top. Turn heat off and let sit for about 5 to 10 minutes and serve. They go great with corn muffins!

Potluck Stew

Makes five to seven servings

1 ½ pounds ground Italian sausage
½ pound smoke sausage [of your choice]
1 pound frozen mix vegetables
1 pound diced potatoes
2 cups water

PREPARATION

In a large frying pan over medium heat, put in ground Italian sausage, and let meat cook, stirring it until meat is fully done. Once meat is fully cooked, drain in a strainer and set to the side. In a 2-quart pot, pour water and combine mixed vegetables, diced potatoes, and bring to a boil over medium heat. Add smoked sausage and Italian sausage to mix. Stir and cover with a lid and reduce heat to a simmer; stir every so often as you cook for 30 to 45 minutes. When vegetables are tender, the stew is done. Let sit 3 to 5 minutes and serve; no seasoning is necessary, as the Italian sausage will season the stew for you.

✳✳✳
Chili with a Twist

Makes ten cups per serving

1 ½ pounds of ground turkey
1 ½ pounds of ground beef
½ teaspoon salt
½ teaspoon lemon pepper
½ teaspoon garlic powder
½ teaspoon onion powder
2 cans tomato sauce [8 oz cans]
1 can stewed tomato [8 oz can]
1 tablespoon chili powder
1 pack mild chili seasoning [1.25 oz pack]
2 tablespoon sugar
1 cup water [optional]

PREPARATION

In a large frying pan set to medium heat, add ground turkey and ground beef, and stir until meat is done, with no pinkness, then drain and set aside. In a 5-quart pot, add tomato sauce, stewed tomato, black beans, pinto beans, chili seasoning, and sugar. Let simmer for 5 minutes, then add all other seasoning salt, lemon pepper, garlic powder, onion powder, and water. Stir well, combining all ingredients. Cover with lid and let simmer for 30 to 45 minutes, stirring as needed while cooking. After it's done, let sit for 3 to 5 minutes and serve. Good with cornbread.

✳ ✳ ✳

Big Papa's Juicy Burger
Turkey or Beef

Makes ten quarter pound burgers

3 pounds ground turkey or beef
1 large egg
¾ cup of seasoned breadcrumbs
½ medium onion
½ green bell pepper
[Other seasoning optional]

PREPARATION

Chop up onion and bell pepper into dice-sized pieces; in a large bowl, combine ground turkey or beef. Add onions, bell pepper, and seasoned breadcrumbs. Beat egg and add to mix. Combine well with hand, and roll burgers into a ball, making quarter-pound sized burgers.

PREHEAT FRYING PAN OR GRILL [300 DEGREES]

In a large, nonstick frying pan, grill over medium heat. Place each burger about 1 inch apart and cook burger for about 3 to 5 minutes on each side until all pinkness is gone. Add bread, toppings, and serve.

✳ ✳ ✳

Country Style Garlic Ribs
Heavenly Delicious

Makes five to six servings

3 pounds of country style ribs
¼ cup minced garlic
½ teaspoon seasoning [Ms. Dash]
½ teaspoon onion powder
¼ teaspoon salt
¼ teaspoon black pepper
1/3 cup extra light olive oil

PREPARATION

Rinse all pieces of meat thoroughly in cool water; lightly season both sides of meat with Ms. Dash, garlic powder, and onion powder. Brush one side of meat with olive oil, then place meat into large bowl. Add minced garlic and mix well; let sit for 30 minutes for meat to marinade. After it has has set for 30 minutes, place on a large baking pan and cover tightly with foil.

PREHEAT OVEN [375 DEGREES]

Place pan into oven, letting cook for 30 to 45 minutes or until all pinkness is gone from meat, after done let meat drain and add barbecue sauce of your choice return to oven for 3 to 5 minutes and serve.

❅ ❆ ❅

Golden Fried
Pork Chops

Makes six to eight chops

6 to 8 center cut pork chops
2 cups flour
2 cups cooking oil
½ teaspoon salt
½ teaspoon black pepper
½ teaspoon onion powder
½ teaspoon garlic powder
[All seasoning is optional]

PREPARATION

In a large bowl, combine flour and all seasoning; mix well.

PREHEAT FRYING PAN [MEDIUM HEAT]

In a deep fryer or large frying pan, add cooking oil. Set to medium heat; cover each pork chop in flour, covering both sides. Place each pork chop in hot oil, carefully, and cook 10 to 15 minutes or until golden brown on both sides. Remove from oil and place on paper towel to soak up oil; serve while hot or let cool down 3 to 5 minutes. Make it a sandwich or serve with sides.

✳✳✳
Cheesy Creamy
Sour Potatoes

Makes six servings

6 medium side potatoes
½ cup sour cream
1 cup shredded cheese [your choice of cheese]
3 tablespoon of real bacon bits
3 tablespoon butter
¼ teaspoon salt

PREPARATION

Cut potatoes up into ¼-inch side pieces; place potatoes into 3-quart pot and boil on high heat for about 15 minutes or until potatoes are a little soft. Drain and rinse with lukewarm water; place potatoes back into pot and combine salt, butter, sour cream, shredded cheese, and bacon bits. Stir all ingredients well and cook on low heat until cheese has melted; turn off stove and serve.

❋❋❋
Southern Style
Fried Potatoes

Makes six to eight servings

2 pounds red skin potatoes
1/3 cup light olive oil
½ green bell pepper [small]
½ red onion [medium size]
¼ teaspoon salt
¼ teaspoon black
¼ teaspoon lemon pepper

PREPARATION

Rinse potatoes well with cool water. Chop potatoes into bite-sized pieces, with skin still on them; chop up onion and bell pepper into bite-sized pieces and set both aside.

FRYING

In a large frying pan [12 inches], put in olive oil over medium heat. After oil is hot, combine potatoes, onions, and bell pepper, then cover with lid for about 5 minutes. Now add salt, pepper, and lemon pepper, and cover once again, making sure to stir every so often to keep potatoes from sticking. Cook for about 15 to 20 minutes or until potatoes are crispy, but tender. Best served while hot.

✳ ❋ ✳

Hot and Juicy
Corn on the Cob

Makes six servings

6 fresh or frozen ears of corn
½ stick butter
1 cup milk
½ teaspoon salt
2 cups water

PREPARATION

In a large 2-quart pot, combine milk, water, salt, and butter. Over medium heat, place ears of corn into the pot, cover with lid, and cook for about 30 to 45 minutes, or until corn is juicy and tender. Best served while hot.

Tender and Juicy Asparagus

Makes six to eight servings

1 pound fresh asparagus
1/3 cup light olive oil
¼ teaspoon black pepper
¼ teaspoon salt

PREPARATION

Rinse asparagus with cool water, pat dry with paper towel, and place on cutting board.

Cut off the end of the asparagus, about ¼ inches.

COOK

Cook on an electric or gas grill over medium heat [275 degrees]; place asparagus on hot grill, brush olive oil on asparagus, and sparkle on salt and pepper. Let cook for 3 to 5 minutes on each side until tender. Best served hot.

Sweet Carrots
Delight

Makes seven servings

2 cans sliced carrots [14.5oz]
½ cup sugar
2 tablespoon brown sugar
2 tablespoon butter
2 teaspoon vanilla flavor
1 teaspoon nutmeg
1 ½ cups water

PREPARATION

Drain carrots and place in 2-quart pot. Combine all ingredients: carrots, sugar, brown sugar, butter, vanilla flavor, nutmeg, and water into pot and mix well. Cover with lid over medium heat and cook for about 15 to 20 minutes; turn off stove and let sit 3 to 5 minutes. Stir and serve.

✳✣✳
Fried Green Tomatoes
Double Dipped

Makes six servings

3 large green tomatoes
2 cups cornmeal
½ cup water
¼ teaspoon salt
¼ teaspoon lemon pepper
¼ teaspoon seasoning salt
1/3 cup cooking oil

PREPARATION

In a medium mixing bowl, pour in 1 cup cornmeal and place other cup to the side. We will use it later. Combine water, salt, lemon pepper, and seasoning salt into the cornmeal in bowl; stir well and set aside. Slice green tomatoes into one-eighth thick sizes. In a platter, put remaining cornmeal [dry]. Now get ready to start dipping the tomatoe slices into wet cornmeal mixture, covering the whole tomatoes, then remove and dip tomatoes into dry mixture.

COOKING

In a large frying pan, pour in cooking oil. Cover the bottom of pan and set to medium heat; let oil get hot and carefully place into pan, cooking them until tomatoes are golden brown. Remove from oil and place on a paper towel to absorb remaining oil. Let sit for 1 to 2 minutes and serve.

※ ※ ※

The Perfect White Rice

Makes four to five servings

1 ½ cups white rice
4 cups water
2 tablespoon lemon juice
¼ teaspoon salt
2 tablespoon butter [melted]

PREPARATION

Rinse rice well, in cool water. Pour rice into a large 2 or 3-quart pot, then combine water, lemon juice, and salt into pot with rice.

COOK

Place rice over medium heat and bring to a boil; cover with lid and reduce heat to low, cooking for 10 to 15 minutes, or until rice is tender; do not stir. After rice is done, pour into strainer and drain for 2 minutes, removing water. Pour back into pot and add melted butter, stir, and serve.

❋❋*

Little Mama's
Perfect Brown Gravy

Makes six servings

½ cup flour
½ small onion
¼ teaspoon salt
¼ teaspoon black pepper
2 tablespoon cooking oil
1 ½ cups water

PREPARATION

In a 9-inch frying pan, add cooking oil over medium heat. Add chopped-up onions and cook until golden brown. Add flour into pan with onions and stir until mixture is brown; add water, salt, and pepper, stirring until gravy is smooth, thick, and lump free. Add more water if needed. Serve while hot.

✳✳✳

Apple Lover Fruit Salad

Makes four servings

2 whole green apples
½ cup almonds
1 small red onion
½ cup raspberries [optional]
1 can of mandarin oranges [8 oz]
1 pack of spinach leaves
½ cup feta cheese
¼ cup raspberry vinaigrette

PREPARATION

Rinse off all raw fruits and vegetables well, in cool water. In a large bowl, add sliced apples, sliced onion, and shaved carrots. Open can of mandarin oranges; drain them and add along, with spinach leaves. Now it's time to add raspberry vinaigrette and mix well; let chill and serve.

✳︎✳︎✳︎

Bananas in Your Pudding
Banana Pudding

Makes eight to ten servings

4 cups cold milk
2 boxes of instant banana pudding [3/4 oz boxes]
2 to 3 bananas
1 tub of whipped cream [16 oz tub]
1 ½ boxes vanilla wafers cookies

PREPARATION

In a large mixing bowl, combine milk, instant pudding, and whipped cream, and mix well with an electric mixer until smooth and creamy. Slice the bananas as thick or thin as you want them.

PUDDING

In a large, flat glass dish, start with a layer of cookies and bananas, then pour some pudding over the cookies and bananas. Repeat the same steps until pan is topped off. Place in the refrigerator for 20 to 30 minutes until pudding has stiffened up a little, then serve.

Homemade
Peach Cobbler

Makes eight to ten servings

2 cans sliced peaches [1-pound 13 oz cans]
2 cups sugar
½ cup brown sugar
1 ½ cups water
3 teaspoon nutmeg
3 teaspoon vanilla flavors
1 stick butter
2 already-rolled pie crusts [any brand]

PREPARATION

In a large 3-to-5-quart pot, combine peaches, sugar, water, brown sugar, vanilla flavor, nutmeg, and butter; bring to a boil over medium heat and cover with lid, cooking for about 35 minutes. Stir as needed until peaches are soft but not mushy.

PREHEAT OVEN [375 DEGREES]

While peaches are cooking, unroll 1 pie crust and cut into 1 by 2 inch strips; add dough strips to the boiling mixture and cook for about 5 minutes, then turn off stove. Let sit for about 10 minutes, then pour mixture into a round baking pan; put other pie crust on top of pan. Take a fork and poke holes into the crust to breathe. Place into hot oven until crust is golden brown; remove from oven and let sit until cool, and serve. Good with ice cream.

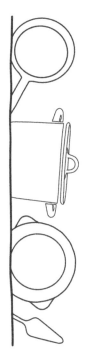

✴︎✴︎✴︎

French Toasted Cinnamon Sticks

Makes two to three servings

3 large eggs
1 tablespoon milk
½ teaspoon ground cinnamon
2 tablespoon of sugar
4 slices Texas Toast bread
1/3 cup of syrup per serving
Fruit syrup
1 cup of sliced strawberries
½ cup of sliced raspberries
½ cup of blackberries
½ cup sugar

PREPARATION

In a large bowl, combine milk, eggs, sugar, and cinnamon; stir well and set aside. Take bread and cut into strips, about ½ inch thick, making about 12 strips.

FRUIT SYRUP

Slice all the berries into bite-sized pieces; place into another bowl. Add sugar and mix well.

GRIDDLE / ELECTRIC GRILL [325 DEGREES]

Spray griddle with cooking oil; dip each piece of sliced bread into egg mixture, making sure to cover both sides of bread. Cook until golden brown; place 3 to 4 pieces on a plate, cover with fruit syrup, and serve.

※ ※ ※

Delightfully Delicious
Chocolate Chip Cookies

Makes up to five dozen

2 ¼ cups all-purpose flour
1 teaspoon baking soda
1 teaspoon salt
1 cup butter [softened]
¾ cup sugar
¾ cup brown sugar
1 teaspoon vanilla flavor
2 medium eggs
1 pack of chocolate chips [12 oz semi-sweet]

PREPARATION

In a large bowl, combine flour, salt, and baking soda. Mix well and set aside. In another bowl, combine butter, sugar, vanilla flavor, and beaten eggs at low to medium speed with electric mixer, until light and fluffy. Slowly add flour mixture [a little at a time], beat a low speed until dough is soft; add chocolate chips and stir, When mixture is a little firm, roll into 2-inch ball and place onto a non-stick cookie sheet.

PREHEAT OVEN [375 DEGREES]

Place sheet into heated oven and let bake for about 9 to 11 minutes or until cookies are golden brown on the edges; let sit and cool 3 to 5 minutes and serve.

❊❊❊

Good to the Last Bite
Peanut Butter Cookies

Makes two dozen cookies

½ cup butter [softened]
½ cup smooth peanut butter
½ cup sugar
½ cup brown sugar
1 egg
½ teaspoon vanilla flavor
½ teaspoon salt
½ teaspoon baking soda

PREPARATION

In large mixing bowl, combine butter and peanut butter, and mix well. Add sugar and brown sugar, with peanut butter, to mixture, then add egg and vanilla flavor into mix and blend well. In another bowl, mix flour, baking soda, and salt, making sure to combine well. Now begin to pour flour mix slowly into peanut butter batter, until all ingredients are mixed well together.

BAKE [PREHEAT OVEN 375 DEGREES]

Form peanut butter mix into 1 ½ inch balls and set them about 2 inches apart on a lightly-greased cookie sheet. Press down on balls with back of fork to form criss-cross marks; place into oven, baking for 10 minutes or until edges are golden brown; remove from oven and let sit 3 to 5 minutes and serve.

✳ ✳ ✳

Chocolate Heaven
Supreme Happiness in Your Mouth
Brownies
Makes two dozen

1 cup sugar

½ cup butter or margarine [softened]

1 ¼ cup chocolate-flavored syrup

3 eggs

2 teaspoon vanilla flavors

1 ½ cup all-purpose flour

½ cup chocolate chips

Chocolate frosting

1/3 cup butter or margarine

1/3 cup sugar

¼ cup milk

1 cup chocolate chips

PREPARATION [PREHEAT OVEN 350 DEGREES]

In a large mixing bowl, combine sugar and butter. Mix well, with mixer on medium speed, until fluffy; add chocolate syrup, eggs, vanilla flavor, and mix once again on medium speed until blended well. Add flour a little at a time, mixing at low speed; add chocolate chips and stir well. In a lightly greased 9 x 13-inch baking pan, spread mixture evenly. Bake for 30 to 40 minutes and set to the side, letting it cool down.

FROSTING

In a 1-quart pot, combine butter, sugar, and milk over medium heat; bring it to a broil and stir frequently. After 1 minute of boiling, remove from heat and add 1 cup chocolate chips, stirring until smooth, then spread over brownies and serve.

❄ ❄ ❄
Soft & Chewy
Oatmeal Raisin Cookies

Makes up to twenty-one cookies

1 cup oatmeal
1 cup all-purpose flour
1 teaspoon baking powder
½ teaspoon salt
½ teaspoon cinnamon
½ teaspoon ginger
½ cup raisin
1 cup light brown sugar
¼ cup vegetable oil
¼ cup milk
1 egg

PREPARATION [PREHEAT OVEN 375 DEGREES]

In a large bowl, sift flour, baking powder, salt, ginger, brown sugar, and oatmeal, and mix well. Pour in oil, milk, and beaten egg. Mix well until all lumps are smooth, then add raisins and stir into mix. Spoon out one teaspoon of mixture and put on a lightly-greased cookie sheet. Place about 2 inches apart, and bake for about 10 to 12 minutes or until edges are golden brown. Let cool for 5 minutes and serve.

NOTES

God
Has the entire world in His hands!

"The earth is the Lord's, and the fullness thereof, the world, and they that dwell therein," [Ps. 24].

❄❄❄
Special Thanks

I would like to thank everyone who shared recipes and ideas with me, making this cookbook a reality instead of a dream.

I would also like to thank the Lord for my wife and children, for all their input in sharing thoughts, ideas, and creativity in this book. God has also given them the ability to use their imaginations to develop new and crazy ideas for foods.

"The family that prays together, stays together."

I would also like to thank the publisher and various manufacturers who helped me in getting this book printed, and onto the shelves of a bookstore near you.

CPSIA information can be obtained
at www.ICGtesting.com
Printed in the USA
LVHW070806080722
722982LV00014B/366

9 781662 849718